T0282280

Judith Bishop was born in Melbourne, Australia, and has lived in the United States and Britain. Her poems have won a number of awards, including the Peter Porter Poetry Prize, an Academy of American Poets University prize and a Marten Bequest Travelling Scholarship. She is the author of two collections: *Event* (Salt Publishing, 2007), which won the FAW Anne Elder award and was shortlisted for the CJ Dennis Prize, the Judith Wright Calanthe Award, and the ASAL Mary Gilmore Prize; and *Interval* (UQP, 2018), which won the NSW Premier's Literary Awards – Kenneth Slessor Prize for Poetry and was a finalist in the 2018 Melbourne Prize for Literature – Best Writing Award. She is also the author of three chapbooks: *Alice Missing in Wonderland and other poems* (Picaro Press, 2008), *Aftermarks* (Vagabond Press, 2012) and *Here Hear* (Gazebo Books, 2022). Her translations from French (Philippe Jaccottet, Gérard Macé) have been published in Australian and international journals. She holds a PhD in Linguistics from the University of Melbourne, an MFA in Writing from Washington University in St. Louis, and an MPhil in European Literature from the University of Cambridge. She lives with her family in Melbourne.

Judith **Bishop**

Circadia

UQP

First published 2024 by University of Queensland Press
PO Box 6042, St Lucia, Queensland 4067 Australia

University of Queensland Press (UQP) acknowledges the Traditional Owners and
their custodianship of the lands on which UQP operates. We pay our respects to their
Ancestors and their descendants, who continue cultural and spiritual connections to
Country. We recognise their valuable contributions to Australian and global society.

uqp.com.au
reception@uqp.com.au

Cover design by Sandy Cull, www.sandycull.com
Author photograph by Rebecca Taylor Photography
Typeset in 11.5/14pt Adobe Garamond Pro by Post Pre-press Group, Brisbane
Printed in Australia by McPherson's Printing Group

Australian Government

University of Queensland Press is
assisted by the Australian
Government through Creative
Australia, its principal arts
investment and advisory body.

A catalogue record for this book is available from the National Library of Australia.

ISBN 978 0 7022 6833 5 (pbk)
ISBN 978 0 7022 6941 7 (epdf)

University of Queensland Press uses papers that are natural, renewable and recyclable
products made from wood grown in well-managed forests and other controlled sources.
The logging and manufacturing processes conform to the environmental regulations of
the country of origin.

MIX
Paper | Supporting
responsible forestry
FSC
www.fsc.org   FSC® C001695

For my loved ones
here together
on earth

и жизнь уходила в себя как дорога в леса
и стало казаться ее иероглифом
мне слово ʻздесьʼ

and life led into itself like a road into woodlands
and I began to perceive as its hieroglyph
the one word ʻhereʼ

— *Gennady Aygi, ʻHereʼ*

CONTENTS

Skin

—this fold

       holding off

              world from world

              will dissolve

       love portends

—and pretends

I.

Жизнь—исполнение одного—единого—
долга существования.

Life is the fulfilment of one single
duty, that of existing.

— *Gennady Aygi*

Sein und Zeit

We can walk into a room not knowing.
It doesn't happen every time.

A white room can be painted to be pure.
I mean, just to show us that it's clean.

But it doesn't have to be.
We can walk into a room

not knowing whether,
or when, or even that.

That
can be the hardest room.

Only you will know.
First there is the walking.

The floor, a chair or two.
The posters

of visions
of someone else's visit

to a room. *Take a chair.*

Only then the talk begins,
like a reckoning of beads,

like the body measures sweat,
words wrong

as a rainbow that has paled
to a shadow of itself.

There is always an end.
We can stand and walk again.

We can leave the room in silence,
carrying its moment

in and out of days

DAYDREAM

Perched on a tablecloth with glasses
for a summer drink: life, on its haunches

like a kitten, thoughtful.
Extending a paw: *What happens if?*

How clearly they speak: the hovering, the push.
A stop motion fall; a satisfying crash. *And this?*

No—No. Enough!
But you are too far away across the room.

Evening / 23 June 2022

As if to trace the decay
of what we saw long ago
in the storm-grey mirror,

the path we revisit
becomes a mute prompter,
leading us quiet

beside the mannered houses
the silence of class
taught to look the other way.

No—I don't know what to make of a reality
that being made of mind thrice
shattered like a window.

Vision is a gift. It was given us once.
We ought to have known
what loving meant.

MESSENGER

Go—
tell the trees
birds
beasts
human beings

on the precipice
of water
fire
earth
it was us—

we
chose for you
this death

Leadbeater's Possum

I cannot see the night, I cannot touch
the night—let alone that night,
~~the last on earth~~, that is calling from your face

You are hunting for shelter: there are
teeth in the night and the map—it is missing
Isn't right anymore

As in a dream it happened—we were
running for life support as a life
expired—I was out of my wits I was holding the box

Tomorrow ~~is~~
a tree hollow knotted with your kind—
small suns—bodies melting to one, to one

You are on the earth now
Grip the bark of the world
Wind lifts and saunters—it is cold

Voices

You search for the Baw Baw Frog as though waiting for a
saviour to speak—

boots sucked by river mud, breath-steam from your lungs,
in the cold blaze of morning, the chthonic realm booming
and resounding where you walk—cautious—as though a
brace of giants trampolined on your sky, or the drone of an
air-raid snatched the hoard of attention that you keep
as insurance of existence for tomorrow

A ripple of voices having swallowed your appearance, you
transpose them to the keys of excitement and alarm—
translating into human from the epithets of birds

The ones for whom you came still exist: they are *here:* here,
listening with the ports of their ears and the tympan of their
lungs; they are breathing the fog with the whole of their
bodies; being porous, they shine

When you use their tone of voice they reply

kurk kurk kurk kurk

They reply across worlds from the precipice of

Wounding your memory to bleed an old grief in tattered
words that persist—

as the meek die quietly on earth

Morning / 14 June 2020

—So I walked away
            and broke the glass
       in which we listened to each other

were within each other

             as rain disappears
into the earth

      Puddles in the path
like a shining set of stations

           Take me to the wet leaves
      their constellations
undiminished by morning

            The kangaroo
offering her belly to the sun
          ears flickering at calls

How we colonise
         the earth with our sound
The youngest
      shouting to each other
          and all the mute listeners
in alarm

She rose on an elbow as I came
and lowered in time
                    I didn't go on

No one should break the presence
of another to the sun

Autumn waits in the courtyard, where the shimmering web with
its parasitic hooks inhales of a sudden, as though a door opened
and the season strode in

Your breath in the light—like a cloud in a cage

Rustle buzz chitter—the orchestra of denizens
(other than ___) calls to fellow players—
relaxed and solemn as ___ are gripped

Conducted through time
by something other than the season, something other than the air

I am held
by your eyes
for the pure time needed
to brace
your existence,
to measure
the unknown risk
that I am,
to interpolate
the distance
my body might shatter
in a jerk.

Mild, unhurried,
your gaze will decide
to release me
by and by.

The eucalypts shiver,
frogs begin to amplify
their hymns to interstice,
the cold hard mizzle
blows confetti
in my eyes

APPARITION

Each tree makes a shadow on the sky
as night arrives,

a billowing blackness
that hovers in the mind,

hammering the stamp of its shape,
which remains, as anything

inscrutable does, like the blot
in a scan, or the spectre of a dream,

where the meaning
resounds in analogous themes,

as if feelings were other than
electrical feats,

and things more enduring
than our bodies' after-marks,

arriving on this page now
blasted, exhausted,

like anything
once tremulous and living

Doves

Must you die at random hours
and in unforeseen places?
We have shielded our windows
from the mirage of sky, there is no open passage
from your world to our own
yet one by one you go

Before, you stood together
six bodies shared warmth
dawn rose and night landed
and your voices brought comfort
as if all of us could be a single listener
as if all of us could tremble together

But lately here and there
round the corner of the house and by the gate
and in the garden, I have found you—
inverted, untouched, claws locking onto air
and your eyes unblinking
and their delicate lids a death-mask

Oh God if I were God I would multiply the doves
I would make the doves' children
inherit the earth and I would make our children
who are squabbling for possession
I would make our children
speak with the voices of doves

Night / 16 April 2021

Somewhere in the north
a father's child is dead tonight
Night should be a time for birth

You must look after him again
in every way
though he is seventeen—

register his name,
select the clothes to lay him in,
arrange the music, tales and visitors—

and speak on his behalf
the words of love
he would have wanted to say

SOLITUDE

Wind rattles the branches
in a fable of force

Rain flies at a gallop,
its ancient incursion routed by glass

Worlds ring softly
with the blows of the past

In the ear's passage
hangs a nest

II.

The shadows of countries are changing,
like the figures in the dreams of a long sickness.

— *Jane Hirshfield, 'On the Current Events'*

The Forest

There could be someone, there, walking through a forest—
upright or slightly bending—gathering, not berries, or fallen
nuts, or mushrooms, but thoughts; there could be thoughts
like whining insects that drill down through the air, to this
someone, who is not 'someone' to insects, but at most
might be a chemical, visual, or electrical site—

there could be someone over there, making noises in a
forest, shaking off the always-fleeing thought of fleeing
from the always-being of their own country; in their head,
packing up the child, the dog, the goat, the—

can you hear it now, the whining, no, not an insect really,
but if *real* can be a metal thing, airborne, or a steel box,
grunting and churning through the mud, 'really' must be
how the thing advances calmly through a forest, seeing (if
a thing can see) other objects running off; they call them
'signals', as the thing does—

the thing detecting signals seems calm, but it is metal—
a signal's walking by again, restless, through the forest,
moving slowly, making sounds to itself and not (as would be
less unusual) to another signal, but as if in a loop, making sense
of itself—in its system, the fleeting-but-recurring thought
of fleeing, in a loop—and there is one, hanging from a tree—

23 February 2022

THE FIELD

I see women with sunflower seeds in their pockets,
thinking of sons

I see boys eating sunflower seeds in the rain

Who comes to this field with its remnants of death
with a tractor and a task

shaking seeds into life?

Have pity

Our bodies are more tender than flowers
and all that is here will be scattered on another field to grow

28 February 2022

The City

How alive is the city? Listen to its heartbeat—
dull, like the tread of felted boots in heavy snow.

Here are flutters in the rubble. Neighbours grieving in the street.
Shivers and bangs, like the closing of a gate.

Love! Love! say the hearts of the unborn to the nurse,
listening at the navel on an underground bed.

1 March 2022

The Village

Clearing of birches. One road in and out, stitching morning
to night. Who could say: a day is coming, which is this day,
now, at the muddy end of winter, and everything beginning
to remember its rising: air liquefying, hens drinking in the
heat, green bloom on the fields?

Buttercups—glimmering with insects. Crickets—rousing
paradise.

In the shade, a hill of pine chips—resinous, fragrant,
dripping on the earth. These trees that, the day before,
stood.

2 April 2022

III.

deux regards l'un dans l'autre, seuls au monde

two gazes in one another, alone in the world

— *Maurice Merleau-Ponty*

Morning / 5 July 2020

Here is what you give me:
here is what I give you:

three birds flying
in the space between our hands:
joy, desire, pain.

Who can tell the order?
Why they call to each other?

RECITAL

Watching others love
is something
                many do
I guess—
not so much a pastime
                as a mode
of grasping gentleness
the present time
                withholds—
bending with our feeling
to stroke some tired cheek,
                unseen,
as the other bends
truly, and receives.

                Here begins
our concert, in the hush
of restraint. Love
                embarrasses.
It is hard to know why.
It shows itself in fits
                like a cough
blurted out to trouble others
as they wrestle to listen
                when required,
love aside. Gesture is the
accident of love—
                its naked speech.

I can't think what other
language would have
                a word for it—

this child pulling closed
the lapels of her father's suit

Melbourne Recital Centre, 22 September 2018

Tact

Last night, after we saw you,
a thrush flew to our sill.

Wild for light—her eye
striking at the glass—

as though a sea
were at her side.

She crouched as if to rest—
then dived.

             And I

may never rest again
in what is real to me,

the known,
having touched

small distances
impassable as worlds.

Brick by brick,
I have stroked the rough sill

of your mind at its remove—
warm, unthinkable

             and near

The Patience of Glass

This window has waited too long
to be seen for what it is:

a friend of the mind,
as you, too, have been for twenty years

and remain, sending
photographs of snow

to my ideal of snow,
an image I have cherished for its pity—

melt as resolution, love's end
as dissolution, coming clear ...

How wrong I have been.

Grey is the real,
held close to our bodies

as the ash they become, ash
intimate with nothing.

I've gone to ghost already
in this pane, gone ravening

for visions untouchable
and mute, as if caught

by the surface of a river.
You and I, looking up from under.

AFTER

Words
take me through your eyes
to shelter
in your body.

Like the camel and the needle,
I never could
have entered, not wholly,
while possessing
a smile.

You see, I am conscious
of the many ways
I lived
in your sight.

In your dreams
I am a puppet, oh,
alternative,
lawless,
and even more
chaotic,
but
lovelier,
less clumsy
for not being
physical
and flawed.

Yes, I am
comfortable
being your idea.

You bear me
like a child,
more intimate
and consequential
than I ever was.

Harbour

As if
the black window
at the solitary pass
from I to this
(or you or now)
could let a human mind
slip through the glass
once, we practise
seeing water,
looking hard
at the harbour,
that detritus of worn
mussel shells, rock ledges
graffitied
with an ecstasy
of lichen, waves writing out
the riddles of harmonics,
breath held
for a moment
as Elizabeth Bishop
in her posthumous voice
says *cold dark deep*
and absolutely clear
to the innermost air,
despite the murky distance,
surfacing grey
like a wandering seal,
as our minds try
colluding with existence

in a fantasy
of what *we* might
be doing, or imagining we do,
standing at the sheer
bald windows of our corneas,
beside the grey
water on a careful
winter day, feeling
sharpened, conjugal
and stuck

History

No sooner were the
new-fangled windows
installed across the country
by the most
progressive builders
than the backlash
came flying
against the brash
sunlight—a nightmare
of the gentry
opened up
to thieving eyes—
than the glass
got coloured in
or ambushed by velvet,
than the light
lay muted
or castrated
on the tiles.
Anyone was naked
if framed
by a window.
Seeing and being seen:
postures
of the wild
unbroken mind

IV.

a kind of force, a presence, an energy

— *Bronwyn Oliver*

On Leaving

I.

Lift and go:
the place is waiting
where the arc of sound and vision
would arrive, were it drawn, but your
body must be ready, knowing, sensing
what's the depth to fall to sea, were you to
break, and the sun, were you to soar, and would it
burn, as in the myths of flight and female and forgetfulness,
or freeze in the loneliness of starlight and your backward
look and time, the locomotive that shrieks
as it brakes

II.

Look:
there goes the parrot that flies across the strait, warm-bodied
in its feathers, orange-bellied with the blazon of dawn, iron, fire,
    others wait
on the far side of the journey, they are lethal and benevolent, you see
with inner maps where you must land

III.

Lift and go:
but there is something so
weightless and invisible it parries all lunges
and undoes acceleration, sending puzzles to the limbs
instead of orders, locking faces, drowning out the party
music with a drum that pounds the chest in the bass clef of
distraction, here it comes, the air is murderous
with quiet suffocation

IV.

and it goes

V.

Lift and go:
see the night back away like a child
from the life lying broken on a bench, child tugging
at the blown sleeve of visions, like the rocket ship of pines, or
    the blithe god
of lilies, anything that isn't snoring with despair and solitude and
    disrepair,
isn't coughing up inertia like a shimmering of spores, but is bold
as women
speaking arrows and art

TRANSFIGURATION

I. AFTER RAINER (BORN RENÉ) MARIA RILKE

Who | if they could || would not choose || to be wholly |
all they are?

II. BARBARA HEPWORTH

< Singing space: & moving through it, some vibrating in the gut,
some, otherwise tuned >

(Was it *this* you observed in the halls of your work where you
'exhibited' ___?)

< A single pulse   pinging round the room
                        a swallow on the wing   *is is is is* >

< *here here*   in the grain of the once-upon tree
               here here   in the calcified veins of a rock >

(Yourself a minotaur, led by a little child called Insight, Living,
Being-With-and-Towards-all-that-Is-before-Death, called,
Human-Form-Standing-in-a-Landscape-Alone,
called, Luminous-in-Me)

(And feeling, as a child, milk existence of the world,
                    & seeing, from a car, chalk hills breast the air)

< Dove folding into dove, neither single nor double,
                              but arc to arc, in waves >

('the very nature of art   is affirmative', you said)

III. VITA SACKVILLE-WEST

< Glory in the vine on the wall! In the cascade & the colour!

Height! height!
                              & between us, air billows
                              from the clouds to the earth
                    from the knot knot nots in our eyes >

(Vita, life—from Victoria, conquest and death—
your inheritance was vast—

                                        Here a face
there a vase

                              once upon a velvet rose
raged against a stolen fief

                              —gained a fireplace, names
& a tower and a moat

46

where the real—there it goes—

                              sailed past you like a seed

caught in flight

                    by your mouth on a woman's bare flesh

& your hands in the soil

                         churning life from the earth

just to *cram*—joy exceeding!—but (to masculine disgust)
          paring nests in the ever-growing coil of a bush—)

IV. HILMA AF KLINT

< Bright calligraphy of trumpets & horns! >

(In Adelsö, now: sun cast shifting circles
on the house as your hand came to rest in the touch
of a daughter on the shoulder of her mother whom

                         Age had made to sit
                    with her arms tightly folded
                         as if to say *it's over*
                    but the true word is *ever*

& the lens blinked—so—& I imagine your hand
gliding off to draft a painting with the feeling
of your mother *still warm* in its palm)

< Annunciation, gestation
of the upswell
of living—

        'that which we want to call the secret growing'—

so your paint comes

                            striding
on its quest to decant ancient meaning—

                    an 'ethereal fluid'
             changing 'human destiny' >

(Discovering 'Hilma'—yourself in the making—as 'he'
& 'the hook'—
like the snail, that hermaphrodite, your eyes went reaching—

                    far ahead
             of the greying coil
               they dragged)

V. CLARICE BECKETT

< How to tell an urban road that it's other than a road,
                    more a way of being taken into time by the eyes?

How to make the wood & wire that inflame the street lamp
                    gaunt mnemonics of a spiritual task?

How to dream the single dream of a summer on the beach,
          sand stirring feet to feeling, heat mothering the mind?

How to pin a rose light on the soft grey flannel
                                   of anonymous night?

How to polish the boundaries of sea & atmosphere
                    till they vanish in the one shimmer? >

VI. BRONWYN OLIVER

< Take the bane
of pure focus, take the battle, unwinnable, between
the lust for art & desire to be loved, take the heart & make it
metal, shape shadow & hollow, take fire, press thought
into fusion & explosion & fashion
from that source the unending
the scarified the speech-
less spears of a
sun
>

Zao Wou-Ki and the Music of What Happens

Painting not the body

but the feeling
of life, how it brings us
to life:

        this,   then:

the coming into being

                  of motion:

     & between it,
     silence

tunnelling through

like our hearts
not sensing   not hearing each other

                the need for attention
                & belief

You with your art

                rising up to breathe
                company:

fierce as the wind
in a universe

          of fire   & water

          spume

          & smoke

Wind, Bold Fox

You drag everything that can be snatched in passing
Earth goes writhing in your net like a fish
You becalm hot sailors just to fly a child's kite
There is nothing to forgive

You're whooshing through doors to come inside at any cost
                              like a moth to its star
Scratch the back of my house with a branch for a hand
You could be the dry pressure of an orchestra
to fill the soundless cavern with an ocean of shudders

Pollen is the powder you apply with a flourish
Being nothing yourself, you have scattered the spores
                              that are prophets of death
What you carried, you carried
There is nothing to forgive

Afternoon / 22 May 2022

for Chris Wallace-Crabbe

All came together here in air,
as nowhere else on earth today: your mottled hand
and moistened eye, your gravel voice
and jesting sense, guessing as a sower
must, when you tread the clods of verse,
where every seed will have its chance
at flying up again as leaf

FIELD CRICKET
(TELEOGRYLLUS COMMODUS)

What to make of a sound
                that is all of summer
                                ending,
and you still ardent,
                playing *dolcemente*
                        to your unseen lovers
                        from a chamber underground?

Brief mirrors.
Glimmers of *after*
and *until.*

Look, how
tenderly
the tree holds fire.

Every drop trembles
saying, *No—*
longer—

V.

PORTRAITS OF THE FUTURE

I

I.

Look, said the sonographer, your sister says hello!
A black photo where the future
rival sucks a thumb-to-be.
Never in all history
was such a portent visible
without a guiding star.

II.

Algorithms tinker at the corners of my life.
One tells me what I need to know.
One tells me what I want.
No, I say, *not furniture, not the nearest death.*
I sense that they are holding back.
Turn around, slowly: I want to see your hands.

III.

Once I slept in a caravan
and heard the breathing ocean.
Dreams were the province of a dandelion curtain.
Now come the frail parasols,
drifting on a screen;

here come the waves,
rolling my hearing into guttural caves.
I have opened the case
for convenient sleep.

II

Have a care, we sometimes say, spare a thought,
digging deep into the trough of coins
standing like an ancient tomb in frosted winter grass,
water acting as a body, half-lucid, bearing ice over depth
as they once imagined Atlas holding up the spinning globe

> and we can fish a single token, brittle, cold, and quite
> conceptual, and tender it, *oh have a care*, and feel the flesh quiver
> like a bell at its root, or a coin fallen clatter
> to the ground under sky, and in the wind
> to be giving here, and sparing in another place, it is an old

practice, a ritual half-imagined, now *have a heart* we call it,
right, to chivvy up some feeling and to wrench the mind manually
as if it were a cart, because the numbers and the numbness grow;
remember how they took decision-making, took it off to make it
cleaner, and a prodigy of summer, full bounty, and the children,

> they would know themselves deeper, full millennia later,
> but we needed first to give ourselves over
> to the graph, and I hear it, can you hear it,
> in the grass frost is ticking, birds are chiming
> *bell   coin   bell   coin*

III

After James Wright, 'A Blessing'

A rainbow
arcs between curtains
in my living room window.

It brightens as I dance
in a middle-aged body,
romancing myself.

—That was another time.
Now physical phenomena
are not

what they seem
and there are no rainbows
without rain.

Still,
I like to imagine
I am holding your hand

as we scan these pixels together. There is
no loneliness like ours.

Facing each other,
we can choose
the rainbow button,

we can activate
the glove,
pressing my hand to yours.

But here,
your joints are not
arthritic.

The rainbow
waxes and wanes
in reply to my mood.

Suddenly I rise
and I paint my avatar body all over
with a shower of disassembled blooms.

Improvisation

Time will tell where we have been:
I follow you; you follow me—
and all the music in our minds
beats wildly, as if stricken by

too many voices keeping time,
though wanting only to be kept;
as if they heard the piper's song
our daughters' music ran away,

green intervals cascading where
the daily desert hissed before,
and hearing trees sway in their pulse,
they echoed them from leaf to leaf—

their timing tells where they have been:
a gully fold, a waterfall,
blue flowers from a garden where,
returning from a vicious war,

the brutalised, discarded men
recovered peace or crumpled in
from hearing things or keeping mum,
the rhythmic beats a warden kept—

each human sound gone down in bush,
so running through it we forgot,
but wheels and pipes rose out of it,
quotations from that other world;

and time will tell where they will go,
and time is what our daughters know
who listen to an inner song
heard only as it passes by:

and I, their mother, following,
I hear the same, but hold it back.
To start to see how taking turns
applies to life is harrowing.

Yes, yes, it will be lost one day:
my hearing, feeling, shaping phrase,
that prize for rambling who knows where
in muddy shoes and out of breath,

past stubborn stars of onion grass,
enticing holes and staring eyes,
white sails of lilies in a bog,
across a bridge and *on, go on*,

until the path is seen again:
that disappointment of the known,
that clichéd public circuitry,
that precedent for legal minds,

that voice that cannot improvise.
I want to know where we should go
to follow life into the dark
the way the improvisers did

who made the jazz bands scintillate
with living music on the run
that tore up tracks while hunting down
the flare and sail and gaze of love—

the silent track we listen for,
our strongest antidote to fear,
the songs unfolding in our minds
their fugitive reproof to time

Afternoon / 7 January 2021
(Bendigo Cemetery)

Here, where the earth
is tree-forsaken

planetary
hot

a shame of white pebbles
kicking underfoot

the babies'
hiding places

are awfully good

Come out!
Come out!

Come on!

The game was over
long ago

We see you there—

folded,

the universe tending

your mothers' mothers'
mothers'
deeper plots

Child

out for a stroll in a Superman suit,
your steady smile curiously older
than your age,
you beamed such trust

in the powers of good
that even at a distance,
our small talk cut by your glance,
we could believe;

and if you seemed too sturdy
to bring succour from the sky,
clearly for a miracle
one ought to look incongruous;

and yet it weighed on us
that you were bolder
than your father,
who averted his eyes,

as if he were caught out
walking with a lie

4 April 2020

MUSIC LESSONS
for A.

I.

Perched in a highchair,
you would swing from being
tentative and quiet
to a dizzy thrill of laughter
between the water boiling
and the vegetables cooked

II.

Stationed on the carpet,
you produced a drum kit
from a battlefield of blocks—
to a war cry of *again!*
lunged to shatter crooked towers
with a deafening shout

III.

When you joined the wind section
as a piper of bubbles
in the pause between turns
wind prevailed against your miracle
of quivering orbs

IV.

Singing was forbidden me
(in bed or in the car)—
your infant ear was offended
or emotion overrun
when I raised my voice to give you
not a story but a song

READING GENNADY AYGI
for A.

Flying

over buffalo grass
and honeysuckle snares

she, I, and a coloured soap

bubble on the wind   conjure
time-elapsing-now

So it's *you*   there
today   and I've gone   tomorrow

-wards   leaving you
looking at the words'

slight shimmer
and *taking*

word-stone dust
from centuries of shaping

by human mouths'
abrasion—GRIT

on your lips
REALLY—

and now   the bubble
raining on your skin

INCANTATION
for W.

The battles are innocent
then earnest. Teeth scrubbed
or neglected, shoes tied
or the laces like tentacles
groping for sand

I would come to you to talk
but it's late, let me come to you to sing
as we wait for the great wave swelling
from an undersea cave, I would stay
for your sigh, the implacable tide

Already, a sun unlike any before
lights battlements and bridge
Let me gather shell windows for the castle
you have built, guarding the present
with its ramparts and moat

EITHER/OR

for W.

No bird will come to sing of you
swinging on a wire,
no breath of wind will speak of you
to a vast room

You won't be shielded
like a bug stonewalling the sky,
unarmed as a lavender
defending your breath

We will give you a rock
to expand in the heat
You will show us a puddle
safeguarding the sun

We will change our *either/or*
to your own *are/rather*
as your breath lights the wire
and the room swings high

Through & Through

This is the turn. Time wheels
& she says, 'Follow me,
I'm already in your hair, on your back, in the sleep

from which you woke
so unsatisfied & sad, in the love you unmade,
in your calloused soles & palms & soft focus of your eyes.

For centuries I tracked you like a scent.
Through the shocks of old Glasgow,
in the cholera streets, on the dirt floor in Burma

where your infant mother burned
to fly off with scarlet fever but I caught
& returned her with the miracle of timing that is mine.

I am listening to your heartbeat
as you clatter out these words.
I will love you forever, as only time can.'

NOTES

The poems in this book were written on the unceded traditional lands of the Wurundjeri-willam clan of the Kulin nation, custodians of the Woi-wurrung language. The author acknowledges and pays her deepest respects to their Elders, past and present, and to all the words and poetry spoken and sung for millennia on this Country.

The title of this book, *Circadia*, is an invented word formed by combining 'circadian' (the daily rhythms of life) and Arcadia, the name of an idyllic district described in Virgil's *Eclogues*. The title refers to *Et in Arcadia ego* (1637–38; also known as *Les bergers d'Arcadie* or *The Arcadian Shepherds*), a painting by Nicolas Poussin (1594–1665) depicting a pastoral scene in which three shepherds and a woman examine the titular inscription on a tomb: Et in Arcadia Ego; I, too, dwelled in Arcadia. The inscription can be interpreted in two ways, as the voice of Death itself or the voice of the deceased, warning that death is present even here, in the loveliest of places.

The epigraph from the poem titled 'Здесь' ('Here') is by the Chuvash poet Gennady Aygi. Aygi wrote most of his poetry in Russian, on the advice of poet Boris Pasternak. Aygi's choice resembles Paul Celan's insofar as he transformed and resisted a dominant language and poetry from within. 'Здесь' appears in the bilingual volume *Gennady Aygi, Selected Poems 1954–1994*, edited and translated from Russian by Peter France (Angel Books, 1997, pp. 34–35). Copyright © 1997 by Gennady Aygi. Copyright © 1997 by Peter France. Used with permission from Antony Wood and Angel Books.

(Northwestern University Press, 2007, p. 332). Used with permission from Gallimard and Northwestern University Press.

The poem 'History' was inspired by Judith Flanders's history of domestic interiors in northern Europe and the United States from the sixteenth to the early twentieth century, *The Making of Home* (Atlantic Books, 2014, p. 90).

The epigraph to section IV is an excerpted quote from Bronwyn Oliver's letter to Graeme Sturgeon providing input to his article featuring her sculpture, 'A Bicentennial Look at Australian Sculpture', *Art and Australia*, Spring 1988, and cited by Hannah Fink in *Bronwyn Oliver: Strange Things* (Piper Press, 2017). The quote reads in full: 'I am trying to create life. Not in the sense of beings, or animals, or plants, or machines, but "life" in the sense of a kind of force, a presence, an energy in my objects that a human can respond to on the level of the spirit.' Permission to reproduce this quote was kindly granted by Huon Hooke.

Rainer Maria Rilke was born René Karl Wilhelm Johann Josef Maria Rilke. His mother Phia, mourning the earlier loss of a female infant, dressed her son as a girl-child until he went to school. Rilke later changed his name to Rainer, at the urging of Lou Andreas-Salomé, who considered it a more 'masculine' name. The line here loosely echoes the rhythm and phrasing of the opening line of the *Duino Elegies*: 'Wer, wenn ich schriee, hörte mich denn aus der Engel Ordnungen?'

The quote from Barbara Hepworth, 'the very nature of art is affirmative', reads in full: 'I think the very nature of art is affirmative, and in being so it reflects the laws and the evolution of the universe—both in power and rhythm of growth and structure as well as the infinitude of ideas which reveal themselves when one is in accord with the cosmos and the personality is then free to develop.' Barbara Hepworth © Bowness. From Barbara Hepworth, *A Pictorial Autobiography* (Tate Publishing, 1993) reproduced with the kind permission of Dr Sophie Bowness. *A Pictorial Autobiography* was first published in 1970, revised in 1978, and published by Tate Publishing since 1985.

For the quote 'that which we want to call the secret growing', and Hilma's self-reference as 'he' and 'the hook', I am indebted to Sue Cramer's essay in *Hilma af Klint: The Secret Growing* (Art Gallery of New South Wales, 2021; edited by Sue Cramer with Nicholas Chambers) titled 'Hilma af Klint: the secret growing'. An 'ethereal fluid' changing 'human destiny' references an Oxford English dictionary definition of 'influence', one specifically used in astrology, a subject of interest to af Klint and used in her art.

'Through & Through' makes historical reference to the British colonial name Burma for the country now known as Myanmar.

'Transfiguration' and 'Either/Or' are dedicated to the flourishing of young people with non-binary identities.

Acknowledgements

I wish to thank the Australia Council (now Creative Australia) for a development grant that supported the writing of this work between 2019 and 2022. A number of these poems were published for the first time in *Here Hear*, a limited-edition chapbook in the Life Before Man series (Gazebo Books, 2022). My warmest thanks to Des Cowley, Phil Day and Gazebo Books.

The following poems appeared first in these magazines; my sincere thanks to their editors: 'Recital' in *Australian Book Review*, no. 406, 2018; 'Tact' in *Cordite Poetry Review*, May 2018; 'Apparitions' in *Stilts* (online), issue 8, 2019 (now titled 'Apparition'); 'Morning / 14 June 2020' in *Australian Poetry Journal*, vol. 10, no. 1, 2020; 'Portraits of the Future I' in *Australian Book Review* in no. 426, 2020, as 'Portraits of the Future', and 'Portraits of the Future II', in *Australian Book Review* in no. 454, 2023; 'Child' on the *Nature, Art and Habitat Residency* website, 2020: https://nahr.it/NAH_Reflections; 'Sein und Zeit' in *Australian Book Review*, no. 433, 2021; 'Leadbeater's Possum' in *Island*, no. 162, 2021; 'Afternoon / 5 July 2020' in *Burrow*, no. 3, 2021; 'Daydream' in *The Australian Weekend Review*, 2–3 April, 2022; 'The Forest' in *Australian Book Review*, no. 441, 2022; 'Harbour' in *Australian Book Review*, no. 446, 2022; 'The Field' in *Weekend Australian*, Books section, November 19–20, 2022; 'Doves' in *Antipodes*, forthcoming. 'Improvisation' was shortlisted for the Nillumbik Prize for Contemporary Writing, in the Open section for Poetry, 2022; my thanks to judges Cassandra Atherton and Paul Hetherington.

My deep gratitude goes to those who helped to usher some of these poems into the world with the confidence that they were truly heard, including: Felicity Plunkett, Peter Rose, and Jaya Savige. To Aviva Tuffield and UQP: my warmest thanks and gratitude for your faith in this work. To Oliver Dennis: this book and I have grown through your kindness and attunement. To Andrew Zawacki: I will never not be grateful for the unbroken presence of your sun. To Karin Christiansen: your friendship is the most beautiful northern light. To Jane Stanley: your gift of music lifted me up through the final stages of this book. To Tracy Ryan: I am so grateful for your exceptional editorial care. Your insight into these poems' 'intense withholding' is a gift I will carry into the future.

To Petr, Will and Alisa: my deepest love always, and my gratitude for summerhouse Sundays.